Wanted Alive

D1470043

WANTED ALIVE

Erin Mouré

Anansi   Toronto

Cover design: Laurel Angeloff.
Author photo: Michèle Wollstonecroft

The author and publisher are grateful for the support of the Ontario Arts Council and the Canada Council.

Made in Canada for the
House of Anansi Press Limited
35 Britain Street
Toronto, Ontario   M5A 1R7

Canadian Cataloguing in Publication Data

Mouré, Erin, 1955–
    Wanted alive

(House of Anansi poetry series ; HAP 42)
Poems.
ISBN 0-88784-097-3

I. Title.   II. Series.

PS8576.0892W36   C811'.54   C83-094166-5
PR9199.3.M68W36

Acknowledgements

Branching Out
Canadian Dimension
Canadian Literature
Centrefold (Banff)
Descant
Fiddlehead
Fireweed
In Struggle
Island
labour/le travailleur
Matrix
NeWest Review
Northern Light
Praxis (USA)
Prism international
Quarry
The Camrose Review
The Malahat Review
This Magazine
Waves
Writing Right: New Poetry by Canadian Women, ed. Douglas Barbour/
    Marni Stanley (Longspoon Press, 1982).

Harbour Publishing, for permission to use 'Fantastic World's End',
'Flag', 'Mr. Hyde', 'Shoot-Out', 'Snowbound', 'Tricks' from the
sequence entitled *The Whisky Vigil* (Harbour Publishing, 1981).

Vancouver Industrial Writers Union (VIWU)
Andrew & Ken
The Half Resort when I was sick
Coffee

Notes on Poems

Zossima Speaks To Aloysha Karamazov At The Wedding Of Cana: Found on pages 379–80 of the Modern Library edition of *The Brothers Karamazov* by Fyodor Dostoyevsky, translated by Constance Garnett.

Evangelismos: Found in George Seferis' *A Poet's Journal: Days of 1945*–1951, translated by Athan Anagnostopoulos, published by The Belknap Press of Harvard University Press, 1974. The poem rearranges material found in the entry for Monday, November 10th, 1947.

MTX: is methotrexate, a drug used over the past few years in chemotherapy treatment of cancers of the bone and blood. It kills cells during their process of reproduction by interfering with DNA replication: it replaces folic acid, the cell accepts it as folic acid, it kills the cell. After the fast-reproducing cells (cancer cells but also, by side-effect, some stomach lining cells and hair follicle cells) have been killed, a drug called citrovoran is administered in a process called "citrovoran rescue", to neutralize the methotrexate and prevent it from killing further healthy cells. MTX holds both death and life; what can kill you is also the same thing that has come to save you.

In The Brief Intervals Between Their Struggles Our People Dream: J. Frank Roberts was president and chairman of the board of VIA Rail, and Jean-Luc Pepin was the federal minister of transport (Liberal), in 1981; the last Super-Continental ran on November 14th of that year out of Vancouver.

Contents

Beatitude

The Desert Instinct

Heat This City

Subliminal Code

Sometimes up in the mountains we get the 'black snow'.
It's an hallucination. It comes when you feel
you are dying on the pedals. You go past
pain, of course. You just think of what you lose if you give up;
you think of all those wasted miles, wasted pain,
and you say to yourself, 'I must get to Paris.'

Hennie Kuyper,
Dutch veteran of the Tour de France

Beatitude

Fantastic World's End

What else can you do, faced
with yourself   day in & out
The bottles near you, a sense
of accomplishment burned in your dream:
Out of bottles you pour   the sad
huzzahs of strangers, filling stomachs & tongues

What else can you do:
the damaged brain knocks on the room's face,
the room falls down,
the Christ crawls back into his mother's soft womb,
bleating like a lamb

It's said there are
those who don't know the self's refusal,
the gravity that nails the tongue shut like a shoe,
the force, whatever it is,
that halts the hand's caress
& makes us civil, empty-headed, sentient   beings

What hate is,
what fear is,
to feel the same ache pushing
the engine of the ribs with its heart like a motor,
to see the world end   in your room among
the stood-up knives
Your belly dogged by alcohol
Your frivolous heart-beat, out of time,
armslength from any   other

It pushes you like a sore friend
into the stopped windows of your body
Where you drink until the dream   shuts its face
& goes away
Until, amid the spill of nightfall,
you stagger freely,
the fantastic world's end   squeezing your bones

Bird

The song builds its nest into the walls
Terrific noise of light   wakening,
released from dream.
Slow scrape of shoes, the day
shuffles back with its fingers & cut scalp, its wet
fussing kisses;
in its arms, a mess of food, an accordion,
the chairs toppled

Outside, the clouds'
grey cover shorn around the trees,
the last wet birds knock their heads
against the season,
their feathers smooth, chirping
    Love me, love me.
The walls sing, taxis spin past, lights glow;
a thin note holds us to the sky

After awhile, we learn to be alive, learn
how the day talks, its embrace muddies the corridor; & tells us
what brings white mist into the road
& thru the branches, birds
                    scarcely visible, singing

Full of seed & fragile wing-beat, blindly,
Their bright eyes free of us
This fallen year...

Post-Modern Literature

Less to insist upon, fewer
proofs.
Raw metals pulled from the ground, cheaply.
Or a woman in the televised film shouting: thanks to you
I end up surrounded by violence.
So much gratitude, Saturday nights spent
believing in it.

But the end of a city is still
a field, ordinary persons live there, a frame house, & occasionally -
a woman comes out to hang the washing.
From a certain angle you see her
push a line of wet clothes across a suburb.
It sings in the wind there, against
stucco, lilacs, sunken front porches, windows
where nobody moves.
But carefully.   All of it

made carefully, children in snowsuits
after school, appear in the doorway, carry
their tracks shyly.
& you at the kitchen table - your empty
bowl streaked by the spoon, the meal's
memory, papers, juice in one glass, whisky
in another, unwritten greeting cards,
a watch, applesauce, small white medallions.

As if saying the name fixes.
As if the woman will come out again, & pull down
an entire suburb with her washing.
As if the city *could* end, in a field or
anywhere.
or if the woman on the bright TV could
stop saying *thank you*.
or you, saying "like this", & pointing shyly.
Too much paper, the children
in their snowsuits holding doorways, white snow,
parrots, singing smuggled information, the corporation gone to

Guatemala.
Leaving Father, the curling rink, a woman dressed
in grey parka & the nearest boots pulling
stiff clothes away from the weather, the back road, post-modern literature

It Is Only Me

for Aline Kouhi Klemencic

Say there is a woman
in the locked-up cornfield.
She is making a desert for herself, not me.
Like the poet said: Fumbling the sky's queer wires,
asking for
mercy, abstract collusion, a kind of awe;
she hikes across the frozen furrows in mid-November
ready to observe nearly anything,
self-consciously, as if the turned dirt
would see her singing,
would answer with arguments on Kandinsky & Klee.

At least she can't hear
the saxophone playing scales in the next room,
taking the colours out of the air;
they become discordant sounds & no longer answer.
The words stay silent on the page, their usual selves,
picking lice from under their collars,
not yet torn, or interested, or censored,
or even free.
There are never enough groceries, does the woman
know this in the strange field?
Probably she has thought of it before, a few minutes,
but now the long furrows
are turning her over & over, like a leaf
in the wind.

Never mind the sound,
the saxophonist is in another country, its mountains
stop him from reaching her.
It is only me, with my bad language, my long distance whisky:
I see her far away, it is very cold, I am
calling her out of her field.

If You Find It

In the morning your skin argues on & on,
pulling the dream away.
It wants your choice, your wise intention.
It reminds you to pick up apartments on the way home,
go to the polls, & buy
a pound of sausage at the butcher.
It sings around your head like a dome
barren of frescoes

Your skin is the hallway in which
no service is ever held.
The ministers were badly compensated, vandals
worked over the neighbourhood,
the drunks sang to themselves, *Tipperary* for example,
even the hallelujahs got sick of it
& moved

After all, no one comes to fix
your lawn on Tuesday, to nail kicked pickets
back to the fence,
to cook savouries in your kitchen, humming,
the *Ave* for example.
You are miscalculated, a bad reading, out
of line with the architecture, your citizens
don't vote in elections,
they twitch & fidget & wait outside for the pub.

& your skin gone upstairs
in the morning, angled sadly over the wrought-iron.
This time the choice
is yours: there are
so many other figures, their skins pulled, silly, mocking as usual

Shoot-Out

The woman locks her fingers in the holes
of trees, like
the holes in her face where branches
grew,
her whole head a forest lifted
alone, mightily
As if the alcohol damage was not good enough,
did not pull the beasts
away far enough with its snares,
no, instead they hooked fierce legs
in her openings, & the string
broke,
then she stood in the hospital corridor,
her husband dead finally
from the wound she gave him in her dream

The family is over, finished, like bad television, shoot-outs
filmed drunkenly,
her arms fired wrong in the first place.
They brought her to the Detox
in a yellow cab & took her bottle away, said *Pray to God*,
said *Alcohol*,
said *No*.
Now she walks into the strange garden two hours only
in the afternoon,
the beasts nuzzle her branches,
the sunlight pulls tangles from her hair.
She speaks to no one,
says she trusts the government & doesn't
believe the angels want her,
she has no more sentences,
she puts   her fingers, blunt hammers, into the twisted lonely
holes of trees

Beatitude

I could be happy in a world   populated
by anybody's gods.
The white & purple flowers with their eyes bunched-up
in a park in Nauplion, the village with no hotel rooms, a bit of air,
sun that comes out in the mornings
to lift its light across the lawn.
Today I am happy enough
to be the woman sitting in a lawnchair with two knapsacks,
who looks into flowers thru the scattered
webbing of chairs.
She has only a small melody, thin
as the thread of a spider, with it she too can capture food.
Capture words thru the overseas mail, walk down
the street with its clutter of awnings;
she can pull her boots on, & wear
a blue jacket on her shoulders.

Today she is the woman
who will not inherit any money ever.
If there are kingdoms at all, she has turned from them
to the difficult flowers.
Enough.
This woman is not blessed.   She carries her hands
like a lantern, a city, a sea with bright pebbles this spring.
She is gone from the kingdoms. She is not
poor

15 April 1979

Snowbound

What I am is
a coat that keeps out the cold,
its seams well-proofed
A sheep's raggy fur smeared with old berry

So is the wine   I'm drinking sadly,
wearing fingers into my arm,
rubbing the old skin I live in,
urging it to get up like a woman   & go on

All winter the furnace burns up money;
I go to the bank & home again
bringing more, bringing more
My coat wet with rain,   I shake it off

& sit to the wine again
I can't wring any more sense out of the words
is what it is
What it is is that I can't go on

My skin fits me just fine, thanks
Stubborn coat, I can't teach it the manners you wanted,
it stinks & pouts & works me over
like a snowbound fool

Look out, I've torn up the alphabet!
I'm stranded here with the stacks of empties,
my future lost at cribbage,
the air dead, my husband drinking without me, the TV

jabbers.
My family still   exhorts me to happiness.
I can't make any more, any better.
The coat I am

keeps out the cold easily.
I don't know if it keeps me safe, or warm

Reading Nietzsche

The pitcher with his thin arm
winds up the world.
He is a boy in a peaked cap   called Nietzsche,
Every church is a stone   rolled onto the
tomb of the man-god, he says gently,
his pitch wobbling in the spring heat above the lawns.

I walk near him,
I am the inheritor:
I am as sad as my Mother climbing steps from the basement,
turning out the light.
I have my Father's old anger inside me;
like my grandfather I am jealous of hard earth,
of the house I built   that fell
years later, a home for bees.
On the other side I am the grandfather who refused love.

Also I am my grandmother with cancer, I am
my grandmother of whom I know nothing,
I am cousins who married & raised children to fix cars.
I am the thin girl, too, pedalling a tricycle
madly down 36th Ave. on Easter morning, bonnet blown off in the wind.
Lawns brown & wet, the snow melted in Calgary.

I too was raised.
in the Church that *prevented the   Resurrection,*
by force.
The sunlight hides in my roads, pushes
a thrown baseball into the lawn;
the neighbours continue stupidly with their lives, & I with mine.
Scientists discover cures for   my family,
radiation therapy, shock, inexplicable
paths of love -
                    where one day I saw, alone,
the insistent boy Nietzsche in his baseball cap frowning,
who didn't remember me,
whose reading ruined everything, who hadn't known
Madness, yet

Kisses Not Whisky

Sometimes there is an emptiness huge
as a bottle of whisky,
hard & glass, caught inside me -
I want to fill it with love of the world,
not whisky.

& not gasoline.
Sometimes it's a Molotov somebody threw there, & it wedged
in my stomach, fizzing, the wet odour
of rags choking me, stuffed into the whisky bottle,

ignited & thrown.
I want to take the hard bomb out, & fill its gap
with kisses, not whisky.

You lean your head on me & my body trembles,
sweating, the clocks tick
with our watches & the sink-drip; & the sound of peaches
outside in the tree.
The dusk is silent as a dead woman come home, afraid to enter.

Even the peach tree was lifted into my life by the stars.
The empty gulp that won't fill, you
get up & drink from the tap,
I can't stop your drinking with my eyes.
I can't eat enough, or the right food, or shut off the clocks -
they uncoil my veins all night like damp hoses,
worn out after so many fire-bombings.

In the body   shock-troops have taken cover.
Without whisky the emptiness sticks like a painted door:
I hear the sink drip on the other side, & the peaches rolling,
& a woman tossed in damp bedsheets
unable to reach me, & me
Too frightened to open

Bliss

Bliss on the cats!
Your heaven was suffering for you
until it drowned.
Outside, the cats on the hard fence above the snow, they are
the horizon stepping closer & closer
until distance is just white,
cut-off from us
A horizon of stippled fur moving across the snow, snow
falling even into the ocean,
its grey descent holds us. Without it we are lonely
as a prairie is.
The cook fallen out of the train near Artland,
his white clothes on the track, snow around him,
his body
It could be he was lonely, as an ocean is lonely,
pulling the soft tongues of snow into it,
making its tides alone
Men & their measurements clotted on the shore
Cold surety, dim
beings in their skins, consoling each other.
Bliss on the cats!
They've got away now.
The cook fell not in the ocean but
in Saskatchewan, a horizon pulled him under.
The dream that came explained everything:

Your heaven was suffering for you
until it drowned,   it said
So bliss on the cats,
pulling the horizon like so much cardboard.
He was alone forever, when the next train came

Lenore

Here is the woman hurt all her life
by money, walking away
from it walking away from her, leaving the children behind
with her in the house she bought from Rose
in 1958,
how she took in ironing 8 hours a day & fought
for the pay from that.
Next week, next week, was all she heard.
She pegs the air with her cigarette & tells of
borrowing 5 dollars from Mike at the Legion
just to feed her girls.
& the house not paid off yet, 22 years later.
Still she thinks everyone has money but her.
Rose has money, Bob has money, this & that one
fade into the haze of happy strangers,
alive with money, she thinks

She sees her future self in her mother at Edson,
75 years old & still cleaning hotel-rooms,
getting up at 4am to heat water
for her laundry,
wondering "Is it clean?"
This is Lenore with no money, the future eaten out of her
& the past aching,
a woman once *so elegant*
tethered to house payments & the girls, now grown,
& the aunts who accused her of drinking.

Today her friends anger her; the toughness she's made of
breaks down slowly, & she cries about
money & Rose & her washed-out loneliness
unconquered in more than 20 years, even by the men she held
to relieve the quiet urge of her body
Never thinking of the love she'd need,
never dreaming this far forward,
to her daughters gone from her unpaid dwelling,
to this Legion & the breakdown of caring;
where her fears gentle her & she drinks her Scotch,
lost with us in the cold
heart of her family

Sentences

for *Mary Grendys Mouré*

1

The short & bumpy sentences of the heart.
Arms of a sweater, bumping
other sweaters in the dark closet.
The crack of air let inside by the dog.
Breathe easy, your mothers
have gone away in cars, dressed in furs, to the sore
hospital of the body.
The heart crouches under the ribs, its beat like a rosary.
Your friends have caved in,
their lips are salty, hard; it's hard when
they raise their tongues to you

Speak up!
Your brothers are shaking their father out of the wet
laundry, unfurling him from bed-sheets in the yard,
divorcing him.
He's your father too!

2
The arms of the sweater are   my arms, waiting
patient for the sideways embrace.
The dog left the door open, I can breathe now.
My mother came back & took off her coat,
and hugged me,
knowing how alone I was   & how I cried
when she went away,
to be emptied by hysterectomy

Hey Mary!
Thanks to you I can kiss the salty
lips of my friends, loving them, stuffing my
sweater into them with its wild arms,
guffawing, rejoining
the bumpy heart-tick, my rosary.
My father writes me his long letters freely now,
we talk together about our own name, Mouré.
Even my brothers stumble up into the doorway, a whole
family yapping & not listening,
as if it mattered, Mother –
Let me tell you I am twins with them, holding our arms &
our years up like sentences, coming alive
however apart our births were!

Woman At Chappell

To see her is some kind of guesswork:
Small in the hands, usually deaf, wanting
always to speak the impossible, &
not out of fear.
When she says *dignity*, concealed storms
break open & blow the same snow
everywhere,
wires are downed, power fails across the prairie,
wheat trains are stalled at Chappell, their conduits
frozen.
There is a spoiled colour in the air,
she tries to change it, her small
hands are not enough.
So much of it she has pushed away,
or sucked thru her lungs to clear it.
The impossible is that there should be bushes
on both sides of the stubborn road;
it is finding out
the horizon & the snow are the same person.

There is no sense in shouting;
the woman does not know
anyone,
her pockets are filled with cards & cigarettes,
her hands show the blue hills of blood still moving,
her collar she has turned against
the white hard voice
                    of the cold

Strip/ La Baleine

The Whale is here in her swimsuit,
dancing a pirouette on a side-dish;
as she sweats & dives, her ripples unfold an enormous body
Unexpected,
unable to speak -   She dances her need for us,
her nightmare seas.

A white tide of flesh, she rises   closer.
The Whale is doing another trick, she's
not drowned, jumps
from the plates & jiggles her thighs down the table, her
moist skin glistening

O Whale   in our applause do you sense love?
Newly-wed & suburban, perfectly
rounded in Toronto, your footsteps a rough crescendo
We are the public who
travel near you, awed & aghast at your desire
that makes you dance   jarringly
Foolish
Whale with your huge arms raised in prayer

Is it
the bad air that makes us cry, as you insist? Or
the sight of you, serious
Whale who unleashes   a tide of anger in her pirouettes,
who acts our lives with her hurt parentheses
The pianos still tinkling, oblivious -

The Bearded Lady Tells Her Story Late At Night While Drunk In The Bar

Sometimes I wear my beard sideways like
a cast-off organ, as if I were
a beast of prey returned
from the daylight, with only a few
sandwiches, lottery tickets, a letter

from the department of the interior,
the real one, the stomach
that is shaped like a heart.
Or like a bird with one side caved in,
spoiling without its song,

in the raw afternoon behind
Nick's Plaza Restaurant, among men
wearing newspaper overcoats, eyelids, toe-rubbers, hair.
I stand behind my own beard crookedly,
a cocoon with real fingers,

an identity concealed, performing
for the facade of voices, costly diggers of garbage,
peelings from the sides of hams.
Here in the alleys I am no more strange
than a man peeing, than the woman choking
a whole sidewalk in her arms

who will take the man away,
& touch his mouth with no word of rancour

Tricks

for Trix, a dog

This is a life in which
a case of whisky is one drink.
In it, a dog goes totally blind & no one knows
if it remembers its young doghood,
the smell of wild mountains carried in storm
from the high passes

I feel I am in the world & there is no god in it with me.
These days my husband gets up & sits
on the edge of our bed & says
a case of whisky is one drink.
He says there are glasses as big as women filled with rye & he wants
to marry one.
This is what I listen to, no wonder
I can't sleep.
Faintly
I hear the heart-tick of my old dog in Calgary, 800 miles away.
She sleeps on the porch, & shies away when the footsteps
come, crying gently.
When there are no footfalls, she rests & waits to die.

I want to leave my husband & let him marry
all the bottles in Vancouver,
while I go to Calgary to sit beside the blind dog of the family,
her eyes muddy with cataract,
& tell her of her old/young doghood, of hikes to the ice-caves
with a black pup in '71, who was herself
splay-legged on the fireroad.
I want to tell her she is a dog who loved the mountains,
& she should be proud even in blindness
that she saw them & climbed their hard trails,
& camped there with the humans
like a god.
Now she is only afraid, of being stepped on.
She knows our voices, even mine that she hears so seldom.
She speaks back in her small voice
& snuffles nearer.
I wish she would remember & be proud, but she lives
only the present in her dogged blind way,
fighting the back stairs.

Without her memories I am alone in the world, the god gone out of it.
My husband murmurs over, *the root is still there*,
in the whole world there is only whisky for one drink.
No wonder I can't sleep.
No wonder to look at the world is to go blind in it

In The Present

In the present she saw the snow
as if it would only haunt her   from outside,
as if she were travelling thru it,
the train rocking, her skin loosening on her bones,
aging & older
The snow caught, coloured the trees,
green trees turned grey,
not even the thin sap
moving
Things that made her life
ordinary, in spite of all effort,   her years of storm,
the landscape mirrored in her,
her own trees darker, unclimbable
She knew little enough   without speech, that decorous animal

The air a loud space the trees can't fill,
she hears
her exhaustion rush on & on like the snow.
Children speak to her, caress her with tongues,
pale-coated offerings.
She wants to erase the storm by pulling the children into it,
she wants her life to keep driving like a train, an
enclosed universe on a metal rail,
stopping day & night to put off passengers,
on worn platforms of cities, hushed & beating as the snowed-in stars

Simpatico

We are all aberrations, says the woman here
Her chair shines straight behind her spine
A white-turreted spear of light
a fragrance of basil
We are eating
Greek food somewhere in Canada, in Kitsilano, on
4th Avenue across from the carlot,
sophisticated, bearded
with jewellery, cigarette lighters, sweaters, or hair.
Always the bouzouki music enchants us,
we can't hear the carlot,
the buses, the road;
here we swallow souvlaki & our university
years,
our own special rapture of liquor & food & sexual
longing, where the waiter John
insists *you know Barb Swail*
& the woman behind adjusts her legs & squacks of aberration
Us, errata,
loud & smoky, shut off
apart from our city
where real people   have a roof & a door,
& go inside, shutting up, sometimes hungry,
sometimes dinner is not what they ordered
Sometimes people can't buy enough to eat
in this neighbourhood, which is
normal   not an aberration, not
poetry, & not the end of this –

So we order bougatsa, drunk on our longing
The waiter's skin close & fragrant
Yes, I say, *Swail is a friend of mine*
Behind us the woman rubs the white of her thigh, talks now
of skylights, hidden,
the sky in them   delicately moving

Shot

There are only so many fears.
That enough of my body is shot away
leaves me giddy, & you –

begin to recognize me again, on corners at mid-day.
Being driven in a fast car is a little
like nothing else, you said,

except owning it.
So I am happy enough, I suppose, finally
recognized on corners,

which pleases me, a good proof.
Human being is inherently   not much, after all,
even to look at

as it always is, wanting
replies to questions, an eternity to go to,
wanting to be satisfied.

The body drives thru the world of things,
pulling them closer, it thinks, giddily.
The things don't care

The body is shot to holes

The Desert Instinct

Grande Prairie: So Far From Poland

Gone to my grandmother's house in the gully,
white light of summer shocked the air into bright being,
all I remember is green
& my grandmother standing out in the shade of huge cabbages,
open as mouths,
manure packed smelly around the roots,
gurgle of wet creek behind.
I followed wild rows of the yard to find her,
she talked the guttural words I did not know & lifted my small bones
over the cabbages, against
her wide apron of flowers.

From her arms I could see the gully, & my brothers arriving,
running along in their shorts & toy pistols,
the ground solid & green everywhere, hot-smelling,
the air steaming
white
What she would tell me, & I couldn't answer, just shied away
stupid & went back to the toy pistols,
the shouts of my brothers,
running faster than the heat in the garden
to keep cool,
as she stood & watched us, worried about creek-banks
& the mad growing cabbages,
locked forever in her language that she brought so far from Poland,
stockpiled like a garden, where she stayed
& did not grow out of

Divergences

*"I am of today & of the has-been; but there is some thing in me
that is of tomorrow & of the day-after-tomorrow & of the shall-be."*
Zarathustra

I am the youngest in a family of boots & shoes
I am the youngest lifting its burnt flag above my head
into the ocean,
recoiling a bit at the cold kiss of water
I am part of a long family lifting its boots out of the mud.
The family sighs in front of me, I watch the backs of
a thousand children growing gaunter, beckoning me.
I follow them for years & years, forever
arriving.

I am the youngest child of a family that cries its body to sleep,
all over the world
Its body unconscious in Argentina after questioning,
shot in Zimbabwe with the shout of joy caught in its mouth,
arrested in Lisbon for *insulting the President*,
gassed in an Afghani hill-town.

Also I am the youngest of a long line of gunners, of proud
trigger-pullers, maintainers of public order,
of supporters of the safety of the state, of the increase
in production: I am the youngest dressed in
white   carrying the Host in cathedrals, singing the glorious anthem,
Singing birth & resurrection for   *those who are*
with us

Friend, are you with us? Do you love your
patron with his feudal beneficence, with his
godly benediction, with his new clothes, his whisky & wine,
his descent into the dead

where he found you? Robber, he robbed you.
He took you out of the dead   into the world where you are now,
stumbling with your ancestors, your predecessors, kissing the
lovers who left you after one night, the passengers of trains—
who walk in front of you in their boots & shoes,
a family.

Family of which you are youngest, barely born, carrying
the same old flag into the sea.
Your eyes pressed open, a light fills them credulously,
the ocean laps at the dryness in your bones.
Is it true you can't go back now?
Go on, says the flag, its burnt edges singing
at the touch of cold water.
Yes, say the family, *yes*, say the boots & shoes,

Go back, cry the gun-shot wounds, opening -

Wedding, Winnipeg

Sunday, late afternoon, the sun
crawls up
across the stone, up the church-steps to the doorway,
white dress of light bunched in its fingers;
a guest uninvited to the wedding, it is
the woman who was shunned, not married,
crying
   Estuary, sanctuary, mortuary, love!

The woman wants
to interrupt everyone with her fears;
she carries her own ceremony, a coat-hanger; her arms
stained & tangled with
hallelujahs, moans; yet on the steps & altar
she is the light,
the woman who wants
to pour bar whisky into the wedding punch, she says
Congratulations, it cures even
bacteria, bath-soap, dreams of the uterus, empty of knives.

The afternoon stone-cold, the wedding gone, the day:
the woman shakes
light from her white folds; this time
she wants nothing.
She is only the sun that sprawls
wide-legged at the gate
of the church, whose steeple pulls its light
across the wall, the prairie
sameness
of decision & love & stone that

insists on Monday,

insists on the factory, nightfall, jokes of
the wedding night, buddies down from Thompson, tables full of beer –

If You Could

for Ken, after a letter

If you could walk into your own
existence with a knife
& cut its black coat off, its overshoes, its tears.
If you could stop the sky long enough
to bail from the airplane like
a stone down on the ice,
without so much as a hockey helmet
If you could walk out of the wooded hill
to the high place where the wind is,
& feel at last the cave torn in your face
that is your mouth, & your own
tongue in it, waggling
Knowing television, the job-site, willy-
nilly;
Knowing the mountain-life, the Chinook & its thaw
over downtown Calgary;
would the wet buildings hear you?
The teachers of bridges, of engineers or treachery?
The women who forged bullets in the last war?
The men of economy?

Then don't do it.
Don't walk, or cut.   Don't bail anywhere.
& Shut your mouth, if you have one.

Zossima Speaks To Aloysha Karamazov
At The Wedding Of Cana

We are drinking the wine of great gladness,
among many guests: Do you see the bride & bridegroom,
the wise governor of the feast?
He is tasting the new wine.
Why do you wonder at me?
I am called too, called & bidden.
I gave an onion to a beggar, so I, too, am here.
What are all our deeds?
Only an onion each,
only one little onion...

Why have you hidden yourself
out of sight?
We are rejoicing, we are drinking the new
wine, come &
drink with us,
the wine of great new gladness
You too have known how to give
a famished woman an onion
Look, do you see how he works?

He is changing the water into wine
that our gladness may not be cut short
He is expecting new guests,
he is calling new ones unceasingly
They are bringing his new wine
of gladness
Drink with us,
now gentle one, do not fear him,
begin your work!

When He Speaks

The sun is spinning in the tree like a wing,
& the family looks up,
their eyes shut to it.
The woman shakes onions out of the cellar,
her hair is just so, parted.
The hard arms, hands tumbled with onions

her head full of dinner, a caught hen
with the string
still on its neck where the boy spun it
over his head this afternoon
How the sky took the breath out of the bird
as he pulled it
down to his mother
Soon

even his father will come back & sit
before the chicken, stewed
until it broke from
its wings
His quiet talk all evening of machine-parts, bolts, the others
no one sees
who work beside him, sparks of metal
eaten thru their ribs
& lungs,
the doors to a new age hinged thru their hands,
Chevrolet, Exxon, United Steel

The father speaks
like this & there is no more sky.
The sun falls out of its tree, pulling the leaves.
& when the father talks
the words are torn around his head like
the chicken in mid-air, before the oven,
before
the child, before the neck   snapped

Happiness

Happiness
isn't my strong suit.
As the afternoon climbs past each of us, separate,
like a grey
beetle on the rusty porch, I watch
my brother playing with the rain, younger than me & not listening,
cutting his boots thru the wide
rails of water.
In the back rooms or hallway
my mother is calling; the storm is passing
by her at great speed.

She is finished vacuuming or she wants to lie down –
She wants to be a heroine in the afternoon
movie, or
to think about cardiac therapy –

My brother is not listening, he is turning
the seam of wet lawn into a blanket,
a hairpiece, pegged trousers.
Could it be this one
that my mother calls?

Or is it me, from my place on the low verandah, listening;
when she calls again
I know she wants to lie down, she wants me
to enter the hallway &
lift her sore feet upon the pillows
in her room among the papers, musty closet, my father's clothes;
so she can ask me
not to be lonely; &
to call my brother, bring him in,
& we watch him then from the window, separate or alive, gazing out
as he carries
the finery of the rain, muddy, exalted,
his heart-beat skipped, not hearing
anyone

Hello

Today they let Granny put her teeth in
for the first time in a year.
They fit like two horseshoes; so Granny gulps
fiercely thru them & says *Baah*,
some old woman's word,
a meaning secret & stubborn, locked in this ward
refusing to tell stories,
frowning at the camera.
She asks for her glasses, the grey ones
she wore to the pictures, when anyone took her,
when she wanted to go.
Now she sits straight up
in the pink bedjacket, raggedy quilt, an honest citizen,
her hair pointing everywhere.
It's Granny & she laughs hard
when you say turbocharger, when you say
literature, just a moment, how are you, hello.

Later, when you say Malaysia, the Fraser River,
Kleinburg gallery, B.C. Ferries, Sadat,
Granny giggles, pulls on her empty toes.
She pushes her teeth three inches out
at you, & sucks them in like a Hoover.
Good enough, she says; some old woman's word.

& when you say DNA, when you say
insurance, Spain, frozen lasagna,
when you say neutron, CBC, Official Secrets Act,
equalization:
Granny stops whistling
& looks out thru her huge frames, she says Hello,
her teeth are clenched in her fist,
& she's smiling at the camera-

Evangelismos

The tiny square of light
the poet spoke of
where so much happens   whole days & nights
a tree pushing its leaves out
above the woman
who comes each morning
carrying hospital laundry in her arms

What is it you would
find then, which existence?
I know only what the poet said,
in 1947 from his bed in the Evangelismos
of a very common square of light
that cut the walls of nearby houses

making them bright.
A narrow pine-covered area,
a patch of slope on Hymettus,
three or four hand-spans of earth
The light he saw from his bed, turning there
again & again with his stitches,

his unfinished business,
his few words.
The light square kept him, its steep
slope severed from reality
past the filthy windowpanes of the Evangelismos.
What he saw held him:

The existence of light upon trivial objects
finally makes all the difference, he said.
It is not a countryside, green & unhurt
It is a corner of light his struggle found, those days,
seen thru the window
of a deeply wounded man...

Westerose

Walking on Billy's land near Westerose, amid sunken prints of
deer that came
all winter to the spilled barley

Walking in Billy's yellow field
beside the willows, their leaves scented & green;
I walk in the rusty light of evening
toward the spring he talked of.
Behind me, our mother dozes in her car; an hour away
Mary drives Billy toward us
from Edmonton.
Still I am walking his land, fields of my youngest brother.
A tall spirit lodged among furrows, I dream
how   our growing changed us, who grew so closely -
The money & speculation,
the turning-away from each other for years
that ends *here*, as Billy speeds closer down the highway
with his girlfriend Mary,
my own brother, & my long-time friend.

& I think of how the years will shape this family,
beyond the sudden shifts   of perspective & loneliness
that displace us all;
I dream how Billy's land awaits us,
to complete our awe for each other's lives
in its stubble, among tracks of hungry deer

Yet I am afraid of our lives
not working,
of subdivision & profit in land, of arriving
& not finding Mary here, unable   to kiss her,
my new sister;
I fear my hard self becoming a manager in Vancouver,
& my mother with her sad dreaming, shut into the car.

These are fears   of a tall woman aging
as she walks the grey-wooded soil, unplanted yet this year,
scaring   birds out of the old stubble;
I turn toward the road
just as Mary turns her car into the driveway
behind my mother's,
& Billy steps out with her to greet us
As I come down from my pasts & futures   into their embrace,
to live where I am *now*,
on the slope in the murmur of willows, the gully
creek-noise, with my family & friend near Westerose, in the tough light of
evening, like   deer last winter, meeting on Billy's land

Spill

The woman with her polished hands,
grew up with a tumour the size of a head,
its fine hair turned to one edge   & exploded.
She stalks
the roadways, her eyes ragged.
Like sticks dragged thru mud,
the trace they leave, not expecting meaning
& not getting it.
This talk of primary needs: the way the woman lifts
her cigarette, stooped over it
like a coil –
Her children are in the alley, plastic-wrap over their heads,
inexistent, doped, fearful, jobless.
O woman with your huge skull aching,   unbandaged
pendulum of bone,
not even your children see you
Standing

at the intersection downtown, muddy cars passing,
flautists drinking whisky in the shut-down bars, away from you,
under the neon.
Once your hands held children, their growing
wore all mark from your fingers.

You are as empty as your children are dead.

Not dead –
Full of chemical, stumped, their hard lives
bestial, winging free of them
The tide of their years flooded,   in the alleys
Their bones spill thru your fingers without words

Asleep Among Us

Between the lamps of the suburb
there are truckloads of refrigerators
that refuse speaking, a program
of infinities, natural conception, remember
your brother nine years old playing piano
in 1965, soundlessly, & you
outside the glass of your parents' house
watching him,
beat of unseen years between you, definition
failed, you waited to fight him –

Now the piano has stopped
& become furniture, the children grown,
on a white highway in the bashed truck, the same season,
the way it was foretold,
singing, not fighting,
we follow hayfields full of pebbles,
a sky that eats canteloupes
before they have spoken; it pushes the road's edge
between the small grasses;
the stones ripening
near us, the ashes of grandfathers
dreaming of the lamb, half-eaten,
carried thru the village on a rod,
its harvest

a ceremony, where mothers with their wired
baskets of bread
turned & argued the future, their voices
suspicious; wanting papal supremacy,
feasibility studies, refrigerators, a list of names:
never knowing for whom they planned,
or who might be
asleep among us
In the cold valley this summer
pouring gas into a truck,
headlights turned to the same city

Desert Instinct

Tell about instinct & holiness,
the spiders on the front porch before dinner,
how the neighbours fear their language
of dark legs, searchers looking for food.
In the kitchen, other spiders
gone down the sink to lay eggs,
are trapped & unable
to climb the smooth porcelain.

Alone on the cold edge, a desert instinct
keeps them away from your hands,
would rather drown than accept those strange creased fingers.
But some days when you get home
the small man, their rescuer, stands
before the kitchen sink & frees them, lets the spiders
scale his arms;
he reaches them out to you also,
knowing them as friends, likenesses.
He who was himself rescued
who knows as well as any spider
the desert instinct.
The small scars on his belly:
his own,   & the doctor's careful marking.

A bloody shirt one night carried his scar alone, on a motorbike
thru Montréal,
in the hands of his brother who brought
its torn cloth to their mother;
a fact, mistake, the present turned away, refused.
This desert instinct, to be wary of his own hands now,
he stays still just long enough
today
to look up & smile at the woman, coming thru the doorway of afternoon,
& offer her his spiders, another day, kisses, a meal
he has made –

Being Carpenter

Then there is the man you always think of
as being Carpenter.
Your brother mentions him in letters, as living
very far away: "Carpenter is disillusioned about nearly
            all of it, now."
He doesn't have a first name, he's *Carpenter*,
he builds a small life of which
you hear little.
            "When Carpenter comes home from work now,
            he lies on the floor for hours & listens
            to the radio, moving only
            to prevent the baby from wandering near the stairs."
This is the latest news.
You remember Carpenter in his muddy boots & sweater
sitting on the edge of the sofa with
his mug of coffee, talking about film,
& try to think
of this same Carpenter lying on the floor in the kitchen
of a townhouse you've never seen,
the radio on, the baby crawling near him.
You always think of him as being Carpenter;
It's hard to imagine any other way.
"Carpenter", people said &
it was a final kind of name, one you could depend on,
one with shelves of books behind,
a film series & a magazine to edit.
Carpenter always busy, Carpenter driving Banff Avenue in his Volvo,
Carpenter sitting on the sofa in his jeans
& plaid shirt, his beard waggling,
animated, articulate, saying what Carpenter would say.

Still you watch for signs of him in your brother's letters.
You hope he has got up off the floor
& turned the stove on to make coffee.
Carpenter is a married man now, & the baby
is growing up as she crawls off toward the stairs.
Maybe he is sad because
he hears her growing.   & himself getting older.
& the film series ending & starting,
& the control of magazines changing hands,
& the extra work of the staff committee.
Still you can't think of him on the kitchen floor, surrrounded
by the mess of late afternoon,
his wife gone off to the studio away from the baby,
who wanders near him.
You wish he would sit up at least, &
go on, being Carpenter, inside of Carpenter's face & clothing,
wearing Carpenter's glasses & beard

Cardiac Grizzlies

At Banff this summer, the river lunged steeply at us,
ungainly beings picking our bodies across the rocks,
balanced incredibly on the cliff above.
Or alone
the three of us hulked over coffee in the Praha
working our way thru the mood
of each other, the speeches.

Sooner or later the rain falls out of its cupboards
& cries.
Ratty wet sparrows in their summer clothes
pick the earth up in their beaks;
when they shake it out
their heads tremble wildly among the cars.
We sit on the furniture in the rented rooms, three
cardiac grizzlies with our huge heads,
the hair painstakingly combed,
the human   well-learned, tho
our talk sounds like leaves that talk
to leaves, on the dark side of the tree.

Our own wildness by the river, outpouring our own banks too,
the feeling of this tangled getting-together
twice a year, not enough
by a long shot but
better than staying alone, in the rough den of our cardiac lives
on two sides of the Rockies.
It's us,   the crazy silent pawing ones, the ones
that crash thru underbrush to keep myths alive,   capable of
finding each other when we need to,
in uncertain territory
Capable of sustenance & love

Heat This City

Heat This City

Tonight
the thought of you   enough
to heat this city.
Surrey, Richmond, Coquitlam, part of
the highway east, & south
to the border.

When I kissed you, after aching
so long, the turbines surged at Mica Dam, & those tipsy buses
wound down Main Street a little faster.
we sat with the dream in our arms like paid groceries.
laughing.   Enough
fooling around, you said

There was some truck about hairspray, herring, bad
& good beer; other
strange talk of tunnels under Peking, dug from shop to house
like a fluttering of hands.
walk for three hours, & no dead ends.
Wait, this is serious: you turned
from the mirror, your face blank with gillette, speaking
of China, its cloud blown us yesterday
high over Alaska.
Debris we never asked for, its half-life shining,
if you didn't breathe it.

5pm was enough damn time; that's why your clock
stopped.   but its thin hand
keeps counting something, oh kilowatts, oh nucleons, oh blue
heart buzzing; when the dream bursts
even the thought of you won't stop its falling, so   Enough
fooling around, there are
cities burning; prime ministers are under arrest-

Long-Distance

for Paul

The woman lies in the
corridor of her limbs
As smoke curls from the ceiling
above the closed doors,
dinners are burning, long-distance phones
are pulling apart the walls

While you zig-zag across the country,
three thousand miles in a leap-frog game, talking
of memory,
I sit in this same room nearly five years,
the walls fade & yellow, the tasks
of daylight redeem no one.
The woman pulls down the corridor with her arms.
Drugs burn in the stomach, atomic rain, delirium

When I'm sad I watch the neighbours
behind their white curtains
They hang bats in the window on the end
of strings,
& cherries, wet singlets, mugs of old tea.

You phone me, I phone you, I phone friends
whether they exist or not,
just to make telephones ring in Toronto.
We are all lonely.
To the walls, we are this much
scenery, the ones with thumpity hearts & thinness
& spirit.
Make-believe.
The woman turns the corridor over
& over in her hand, she hunches between the neighbours,
the tumbled phones ring down the halls, she
waits for you, now

Confines

In the slow confine of intimacy, tell us
how you stood up alone
& pushed the cleaver into the wall, right thru
the calendar, near mid-month just after pay-day,
after rent, the bank payment, & the forty
you owed to Don.
Or anyone; it makes no difference
when you look at the wall now, or try
to chop onions with the broken
edge

On pay-days you are like Jesus, only
a bit drunker,
later you are just a *bonhomme*
who can't pay the price of a taxi.
& I am the tall woman
who keeps a record,
who eats the food out of the refrigerator.
Who goes away, stubborn, carrying
your fists with her, your cleaver,
a loaf of bread & salami, chopped onion

Your intimacy wants
to have public dinners, make chrysanthemums grow
in a basement apartment, to save money
for a house or holiday, a car in ten years, a potato.
Instead I am the woman who
pleads insanity,
who sits in the park eating your sandwiches, who
won't listen, who doesn't want
anything to get better,
the woman who doesn't want to be driven in a car.

The look you had, sheepish, when
you turned around to me, showing
the cleaver you pulled out from the wall, the slashed
calendar.
After all that, the two of us laughing, tell them
How we stood then, arms
clasped knowingly –

Fail-Safe

Our love couldn't have lasted longer
There was a point at which the birds
flew in & gorged on our argument
We waited for the man of steel &
no one came

It was you I waited for
& broke up against when you arrived
Swollen with blood
Your tremulous love   a condition/ medical
Fail-safe

The towers from this distance
dissolve in rain, the acid
of industry   smelters & mills
Holy places
This city is full

We are trace/elements leached slowly
out of a collective life
The city grows up around us
whether or not we go on
It's only we   who can't abide

The rain burns us only when we touch
As usual you're safe from flame
& from the birds, burst   open with desire/
I'm gone.
Fast as the danger passes.
These places are holy.   & glow, without us

Sanctus

in the hall, the same
lightbulb burnt-out for days, marked
like a beacon.   in spite of.
your face with its torn eyelids
spun by the window, fated charm.

i stand in the chasm between night
& the hours, muscles tight before me, like
the fear i had once, & went bowed
to the lucky priests for forgiveness.
disorderly.   needing a coat.
speak: sanctus, sanctus.

in those days disorder
an offense against government.   the army marched
from my language into yours, wielding
their cherished badges.
hold it, i love you.

holy orders, holy war.
citizens taken without charge: mute, raging.
the same light burn-out for weeks; too many sudden
corridors.
hard to speak anything, blasphemous words.

in the chasm, cupboard doors crash shut with no favour.
i'm hungry, but i've already eaten
my fingers.
today surgeons touched the pulse in my foot, & jerkt
back, astonished.
when they opened the speculum, my cervix
clenched.

now i can't tell the truth about events or anything.
there are too many orders banging doors.
too many priests, governments, obeisant armies.
hold it, i want
to sing to you.   in spite of.
get out the chasm & wear it, like a ripped coat,
if they arrest you, i'll kill them

White Rabbit

From the third storey window, you hung
your rabbit from a long chain.
He's there tonight, quiet & strangled,
bobbing a few feet off the lawn.
His fur shows
which way the wind is blowing, or
which way I am driving, up the roadway
of gravel & weeds, if I could drive/

Instead I am standing three weeks from now
below your window, in the empty lot
where they tore down the house beside yours
last week, I guess.
Don't ask me where the neighbours went,
or if they saw the rabbit hanging
& left, because of it.
I don't know, & you
have three weeks to figure it/

Stop saying you let him down to feed him & there wasn't
enough chain!
Your story doesn't wash & I'm sick of it.
For three weeks your rabbit has been hanging from that window
without saying a word, or even touching grass,
let alone eating it.

I'm going away myself
in a few minutes, never mind where.
Three weeks from now you'll see me turn
from your window & walk off across the darkened lot,
I probably don't even have busfare.
You can watch me as long as you like.
It doesn't matter.
Even when I don't see your window, I see
the blasted rabbit, his face is dry & black
& he's started singing a bit, some silly tune/

Flag

for Paul

A thin flag of blood, she wanders
the edge of Friday afternoon, downtown
laughing, shaking her arms

As usual
She has a whisky bottle full
of rock & roll

The traffic spins thru her, her veined arms twist
its threads,   like the clear note of
a saxophone sung low & sadly

Her whisky rattles in her arms, it is the way
of ritual, a bottle with one stone   shaken
over the hysteric body

Racked with the crowd, she dances her desire
A thin flag of blood
upright on the lip of pavement, surprised

Stopped for red lights, unmolested, a citizen,
a flag dancing over the slipstream of hours,
she caresses

her own bones with its heartbeat, the rolled-down
music escaped from cars,
laughing at those who are left behind, shaken & older

Tricks With Poinsettias

Catching poinsettias
is not my idea of winter sport
Or catching colds, or onions, or fish
that climb out of the cellar into the dirty cupboards
Their mouths are lined
with the leaves of oranges, gently
whispering
I have to speak up because even the oranges
have been eaten by huge poinsettias,
the ones you hurled from the next room
toward me,
that I never caught, that I struggled to kiss,
or that broke into red sepals in my arms

I'm too clumsy
for your tricks with poinsettias,
their earth splattered wet against the cupboard doors,
spilled thru my own sore fingers which I am
washing in the kitchen,
which the fish see from the cellar &
make fun of,
while I stand near the faucets & call to you,
my hands soaked in dirt & kisses:
I still hear

your poinsettias in the next room, they have
changed places again, they are
your tough messages, they
break as they fly

Tonight My Body

Tonight my body
won't come home to me, it won't
hug me at all
It huddles naked three blocks away,
on the roof of the stone Chinese church
by a belltower
How its lungs howl out its anger,
its heart fizzes in the dark
rain!

Tonight I am faithless & wayward, I am
my cousin & my aunt
sitting on the shoulders of my body three blocks away,
both of them howling
fit to burst my ears, & me stupefied & cold.
My insides are smeared with warm sperm,
don't talk to me!
Tonight it's my body, I'm stuck with it, don't
talk to me, I'm finally out of the woods
& off the ferry-slip

over the Lion's Gate &
into Vancouver,
my skin lonely as a sail,
I've climbed up the wall of the Chinese church
& left my body angry there
When I cringe
it shudders three blocks away, I can't
comfort it, or coax it out
from under its relatives, to come nearer
to home,
& hear me, who cries for it –

Old Friends

The same gestures over.
Calling the woman up late at night, probably she is
sleeping
with some man, it is
the same gesture, useful
What comfort there is
is at the end of a telephone, the burnt sad
smell of your arms
that held her, somebody else's wedding   two years ago
Where you argued & hit her
& others sent you home in a cab.
Or drove you over the bridge to Vancouver.
Speed is the only good drug, you told her
so hopped-up your muscles would ache for days.
You couldn't have known it then.
Mostly your arms,
when you lifted the telephone, your coat, a letter

& now, on the phone to her again, the same soreness.
You couldn't know yet what it is she will say.
Somewhere, someone
has already written it
Someone has altered its order & sent it away

It's gone.
You on the phone.
The letter she sent, asking you

Fear Me

A city leans its light across the water &
looks in, tipping your window
Tipping me & you
into the tangle of your legs, your sofa
Stop me or tear me away
I hold back & touch you *once in a while*,
to feel the heart in me
tearing
A woman who can't stop her need of you
Who, impeded by desire
won't let desire threaten you, unwanted,
who won't explain, won't
say out loud, physically,
won't admit

I can drink wine all night to drown
to raise the tide between
our bodies
& make it safe for you
The storms I won't speak of, the city
shimmers wildly when I look at you,
a tenderness so cruel, & strange
Toward you, who hold the force of people's caring
including mine -
whose heart rarely sees you, & when it does

goes mad, the sparks hurting my neck, & sides, & breasts & fingers
Till my arms cry out, compelled to hold you
Pulled in all direction, without precedent
Away from you
so you won't know, & fear me

Wabamun

Deciding it is better left alone,
the way it is & has been,
untouched:
The woman loving the man in each facet
of distance
knowing he is older   than her father,
not her father
She feels his faint love for her, daughter
or not, the strange energy that moves between them
as they work together,
as two poles meet & oppose forces,
alive

The jokes they make
ease her tension, he is old enough
to see thru tension,
married with grown children, working the railroad for years;
he remembers
& she listens gladly
A young railroad woman, a new   breed
joining his family she has never seen
The same tenseness continues in the generations
beside them, apart from
the love she has known for him since she started,
they know it & speak/   laugh mostly,
glad

that this much, at least, between two people   is possible
& can be opened
each time they meet on trains, & worked thru freely,
believing in time-warps, nights   where the stars move,
the train passing Wabamun, the distant
other worlds

Firehall # 3 : Heart On Trial

Today I stand at my window & watch
the firemen pick up hoses with their young arms
Blue-shirted,
mustachioed, in love with the ordinary
tedium, a precision-ballet of work & ladders,
their practice of rescue,
the red brick housing them.

I miss you more than ever.
                          My heart too
is the red brick, its fertile cells moving in & out,
re-stringing the veins,
counting them, laying the arteries in neat rows,
uniformed, young & sexual
tho the job is ordinary, & the same.

With them I wait to break   out of the red brick
to the fire,
the sirens blazing
Flame dancing again   outside my body,

where you are.   Or
one like you.
Your replacement.
My fire.

Mr. Hyde

"He sure is a stubborn man." Cabbie

There he is, the stubborn man, walking down the street
into a headwind of his own self,
slanted,
shoeless at midnight,
his bare feet pull the pavement into staggered waves,
he lurches   drunken   thru the shade of trees, he thinks

In the dark of the road, a woman
opens the taxi door & shouts without obscenity;
the headwind of the man drowns out her words

Even the poem hears nothing,
is deafened.
Even the woman is in the huge shade of midnight,
the roof-light of the taxi shines on her bones, they show up
an eerie x-ray.
Only her love is missing, the chemicals break it down,
it dissolves.

Still the man walks, his feet make stubborn hits
on the pavement, he crosses the corners
a little wobbly for his age,
as if the headwind is a sort of tornado, a dust-storm with no dust
but that of the spirit,
spun thru his limbs, thick as alcohol

This is the stubborn man, made by the stubborn man,
tho he had no inkling
Hey science! The woman calls & gives up, gets out of the taxi,
as the headwind pulls
her heartache far away, into her unlit belief in him,
the man, Mr. Hyde, *the bad-deal man*, gone
home alone,   her lover

Her Answer

I am not the delicately-boned
woman   who sang to you in your fine dream

But the one who came,
wordless, mortally saddened,   when you woke from it

Subliminal Code

Subliminal Code

Across the screen, the white hands
of the dead man flutter, this is perfect
art; as he tells of terminals, sickness,
huge bodies possessing him,
the hands falter & rise, attending
his words—

In subliminal code the hands signal out
a window we do not see,
the camera's struck vision refuses it, or us,
watching:
as the hands call the buds on the trees
to burst open, the dead man
speaks of satire, disease, those who came
laughing at it; & how
the bodies became part of him, growing or
singing, in their outsized overcoats, their unwieldy clothes,
their tricks with minerals & wine.
He talks of losing
control, wanting the cures;
& of the day
he stopped believing in streets, taxis; now

his hands shudder white marks on the screen, the trees
burning around us, his hands enter the leaves, strain
to listen; they want to insist
something to a stranger at a cross-walk in Ottawa, L.A., Edmonton,
Vancouver, now
there are no more taxis;
his hands white leaves shimmering, push the cameras away,
finished, to a place
beside his ear, listen, on the bright screen
the hands of the dead man moving
spell

Why it is possible, it is, why
possible—
That the leaves burn so long in the trees,
they flicker & will not   go out, refusing this:

MTX:

In memoriam: D. W.

all of us stand
stupidly in the same traffic jam,
you waiting for your brother with
the funny name, ready
to ask him for the message.   me, i'm
at the gap, dressed
like a friend, you do not know yet
how to destroy yourself, i wear
your brother's coat, i am not
poison, i am here
to bring you the wrong message
soon.
give me one break,
one kiss.
like a friend, your body does not know yet
how to save you; i am in your brother's
coat, i am here
to twist the code in you, the one
you ask for, & your brother gives you daily,

now you stand in the traffic
in your crumpled hospital shirt, waiting
for me, saying
                    DNA! DNA!

my answer: i am coming to break
your code, are you ready
to embrace me?
from the traffic of blood, the alien
cells with blunt faces teeming,
their confused generation stopped;
from the traffic of words, feel
my acid kiss, rescue me!

The Alleys Of:

The alleys of my dreams are filled with
false moustaches,
vendors of cigarettes, can-openers, keys
When the prime minister phones them
my dreams are convinced
of the unworthiness of politics; their alleys
are full of blackmailed ministers, secretaries
who have spoken to judges,
they totter on the gravel in their huge shoes,
holding the skins of fishes, loaves of granite, & pears.
Their mouths stay
open a little while, it is
a trick of the camera, airbrushed, in fact
no one is listening:

The can-openers are waiting for cases of Molsons,
the keys for doors,
the conductor whom you have not met
for a train of white boxcars to conduct
to Boston Bar,
where his children will welcome him in return
for his paycheque,
where he will eat eggs for dinner, tossed salad,
& watch television, on the Main Street under the lights,
safe from prime ministers

Barrington

for Tony Klemencic

There was the hard day you told us of,
nineteen stories into the sky; with your grey
shirt-sleeves rolled, the metal box filled
with tools, hammers,
fixing some thing on the roof of the building.
You couldn't tell us what.
Or if it was sunny.
If it was the shingles, or something to do with the drains.

You told us you worked with an old man, that between
his hands & the tools there was
no withholding.
All day you tried to work as he did, moving slowly
across the roof like a cat
high up into the daylight.
For you this happened;
for us it is just an image like a film, you & this man
nineteen floors up the building on Barrington,
the light is hard, all your arms move together,
tacking the roof, feet spread over it,

you & the workman high above us in the sky.

Then you told us what you dreamed then,
that the roof was done, you both
had turned your arms back thru the sleeves of your jackets,
& locked the tools, when
the old man jumped off the side of the building.
Holding his box of tools, that evening.

& we see you as you tell it, awake with our glasses of beer
on the twelfth floor of the same building, where you live,
gazing with you
into the dark where the old man fell.
How he fell, you told us: like a lamp, like a skiff of paper,
easily, you dreamed him falling like a seed,
slowly, ready to land.
Waiting for you.
& you jumped after him, you too with your tools.

It was like jumping off a stair, you said, when you landed.
You had seen the whole city thru its haze, the sun
pushing the lake into the towers, the light
as it sparked
each window in your long floating,
nineteen stories to the street & the old man outside the door.

Then we take our beer again, the same grainy film
of your dream runs past us, its defiance of the layered city,
the people in their houses along Barrington
eating dinner,
& your jacket floating, sunset, the hard speck that was
the box of tools, & your wild trust of the man,
that carried you down to us

Driving Underground

Toronto, beneath your streets there is a railway.
It has gone the way of railways,
underground.
Where the government can't find it,
to tell it
Fly thru the air or lose your subsidy

Instead it rolls on, its drivers beneath the street
are enginemen in the narrow tunnels,
seeing nothing, or not much,
the platform entered quickly
& the train stopped,
the engineman stares into the tunnel ahead.
Shifts, years of the same track
without daylight, just the echoed moan of the wheels,
metal on metal, pulled behind

This is what the railway in our country has become.
Cut off, & buried under a few streets,
Bloor, Yonge, Spadina
& the enginemen buried, signal lights & switches underground,
coaches all buried,
the citizens of Toronto dig themselves into the railway
to get home,
without knowing why it came here, to be invisible;
or why, on the last harsh turn
into Union Station, its wheels cry out of exile,
aching for the mainline & prairie,
& the sky's fine light
Empty, above –

Toronto 1981

Radiare

Slow wheels of fear tearing sideways
in your dreams
Your hand caught as if
reaching for someone, after the wall's crumbled
Stunned & unable.
Chemistry mills the body into finer cells,
process without desire;
it builds acid into muscle, absorbs the clear
rain of commerce,
tightens your lungs around it, your eyes

In magazines they write of
the American experiment:
The common field of human endeavour, they say.
Its coloured radiative cloud.

Beloved necessity!
You choose the commerce or the nucleus, dark
& split.
The experiment pushes
the walls of chemistry, gently, hoping

the ones it devastates will go on,
their cells lustrous
& without refuge.
Will anyone admit them as human?
Their flushes, their four hands.
The cell wall.
Push against it.
In the morning pulpy rain falls without reason,
the cut apple-tree sucks it in
& grows green.

Hallelujah: the sun pushes coarsely
across your pillow;
in its light radius your life is measured,
a half-life, an orbit of fear
Still the old dreams recur, even in daylight:
you can't stop
the wheels, or the hand searching for you
before the Cities blew

Not A Train

When the girl hit the train window with the sledge,
breaking it into ice, she
frightened me, I held onto the sledge with both
hands whitening, glass in the roomette bed,
the train tilted, bent like
a moon rocket

The girl shifted & tied the bedsheet onto
the door,   when
she climbed out of the train window
onto the rocks of the river
she scared me
I picked up my duffle & kit & walked up
the twisted rails, my train tilted into the bank &
jackknifed, a moonscape,
the ties splintered, pieces of torn steel:
I was the girl who woke up
just before her train derailed, 245am last August,
her body knowing what was wrong; it threw her
against the head-end of the roomette
& held her neck
surrounded by pure air &
the metal bending up into a branch of light
& fear
That's it, she thought
She knew the world was over, was over, was over,
who was she?

Hitting the train window from inside,
straining her arms against the force of the sledge,
kneeling on her bed, glass-filled,
six feet tall, courage, her second life
opening up.

The feel of it.
The feel of *not being trapped anywhere.*
The feel the ground made on her legs when
she dropped out of the train onto it, & looked back
to the metal she came from,
thinking   *A train moves, I am*
not a train

Seven Rail Poems

1

Fraser Canyon

for the waiters & waitresses

The train wrests
the sun out of the rocks,
buckled rocks that make the light grow
huge on the mountain-side
Trees & transmission lines blazing long wires thru the scars
Above them-
Clouds, fierce & silent
torn across the buttresses & edged darkly
Saw-tooth trees glancing thru their huddled argument
Their song without name
or recognition
Power carried down from the dams
to cities by the sea

Wheels sing against the rail, shearing metal, the train pulls
mightily
snaking down the Canyon with us
caved in its belly
as our hunger grows us weary, weary
Workers awake half the night
in the closed kitchens drinking beer
Sliding arms across each other
Lovers of humans, of steel   diesel trains, of the long
race across the Valley
Lovers of kisses
Servers of food

2
VIA: Tourism

Always, the same bodies
slumped in rows, the same questions & fear
of accident or delay
The words of technique, comfort
dealt out to strangers in the wheels' rough noise
The jagged train of hours

Then there are the women   beaten by their husbands
who bear the marks
as they bore their children,
without disgrace,
who bring their children away with them
across the country in coach seats or
jammed into one berth
drinking pepsi, eating aspirin
Locked in the motion of rails, of constant arrival
Their bruised eyes & hands swollen
from battering tables
Insistent
Children tangled among their legs
Vacant of husbands
Wondering, alone
Gone where they've never been, moving into their lives
with no more father

Above all this, for miles & days, the habitual
tourism that never stops, the PR rep in her blue coat
saying VIA, VIA

3
We Are A Trade

Sometimes people clutter in aisleways, holding
unspent money,
their eyes tired, by days travelled
in broken airconditioning,
the sun & prairies cut in their bodies, their stance -
You can't say you don't see
Pythagoras,
the immigrant Canadian sending money home;
he's out there in his lousy field of rapeseed
on New Holland equipment, cutting
one yellow swath from the horizon.
Some will call this impossible
politics.
Pythagoras will turn his tractor toward the train.
His belief bends the earth & grows.
Wheat corporations take the money, America -

In the train, passengers eat & return
to watch & drink whisky,
speak old aphorism -
the duck-lakes of Saskatchewan, money in Alberta,
Valley farmers dead in their silage
& us, employees, members
of the union who won't vote anymore
who serve doggedly
18 hours every day, who work dogged
For the time off at home, whole afternoons spent
in poolrooms, or sleeping
Affluent in dreams, paying rent in public housing

What do you expect from us
We earn dividends for no one
We watch Pythagoras & prime ministers from the same train
flat & curious
We are a stubborn trade

4
Oakville

It is not the toughness of smoking cigarettes,
of getting things done.
It is tough as the nights & days spent
working long hours, knowing a strip of country
thirty-feet wide & thousands of miles long,
in the heart, where it sticks.
This toughness talks of the crop outside
& the bad years
knowing they pass quickly
It talks of Oakville Manitoba in '76 when the engineer saw
the loose rail
& pulled emergency, & the rail hit –
twisted up thru the train into the sky, & back down
thru the train again like a stitch.
With a brake like that, says Ray, *you STOP*.
Ray in one corner then, all the kitchen dumped over him.
Gravy & boiling chickens.
The diner on its side in the ditch.

I never saw roast beef leave the oven so fast, he said.

& This is the toughness that comes back from hospital
& rides
over the prairie at Oakville twice every 10 days,
cooking beef in the metal kitchen, bracing
white-clad legs,
serving the same meal over & over.
Feel the movement over the switches.
The shadow of ripe grain.

5

Public Relations: Delayed Train   or
The Address Of The President

This is how nerve endings   stop
& turn;
continue as rails swollen-up by the sun,
treacherous:
The electric fibres, diesel generation of the brain,
generation of synapse, thought, the way
the passenger rep snapped at the passenger on Tuesday,
invoked his ancestors,
silent ones with their bones failing.

& the passenger cursed VIA,
howled at the railway, its blue diesel train pushing
the mainline between mountains,
14 hours behind schedule;
& he cursed
the crews whose hands ache with hours.

This is the way the nerve   endings   stop
& burn the slow atmosphere, slow
generation of oxygen, slow crumpled diesel thought
bent under stone
for centuries, the nerve   endings   stop
The train curls along the lake from Kamloops
The passenger rep snaps   *This is the address of the*
                                  president.   Write HIM a letter.
                                             224395

& turns, stopped
To the washroom to represent no one, her throat tight
with passengers,

with sick risings at 4am
in major terminals, with dropped
switches, engine-brakes, pullman sleepers parked all night
in Vancouver station,
her throat stuck with arrivals
at 2am on delayed train #3,
laughing-stock of the railway, its passengers fitful, the crews edgy,
41 hours payable in 2 days

6
What He Knew

If he had been able to silence his heart
what his strong heart knew

Years on the passenger service, fifteen hundred miles
across half a continent, a few inches of globe

He can't tell his grandchildren
what his heart knew

In the pullman sleepers for thirty-five years
obsolete time

Work in the berths four hours
in the morning, four at night, sit out the miles
glad enough in the service

If only he had been able to silence his heart
after thirty-five years of trains
Forcing it

until it silenced him, on his
driveway of wet snow, holding the shovel, a few steps, startled,
Just two weeks on the pension

What his heart knew then
His thousands of heart-beats stopped telling

Passenger Service

I'm proud of my optimism,
it's mean not gratuitous–
I came to it arguing, breath punched thru my lung.
The hole it left, is like

a red flower in the railway ditch
seen fleetingly, a few seconds from the passing train;
after a long summer of rain & unrested
companions, overflowed veins

In The Brief Intervals Between Their Struggles Our People Dream

"#4, you're on the Main..." CN brakeman to engineman

In the 4th setting of dinner, the trees
brush past them, waiters & stewards
memorize the orders, dreaming the last Super-
Continental,
the tale-end of a job after
all those promises

Later, they clean
beneath tables, the diner hurtles into night
where the tracks are laid for it,
its subsidy,
its workers are struggling but still have dreams:

Of taking over, the day after cutback;
if all the rail unions
could stand together
& run the Super thru
against all orders, cut in the cars
in Vancouver terminal, change the brake-shoes;
the waiters dream of
carmen checking the A/C relays,
ticket-agents selling tickets without ReserVIA,
on-board personnel reporting
in uniform
tho they're laid off & finished,
the enginemen coming to drive,
dispatcher & crew routing the Super

out to the mainline,
full of passengers,
its cars shimmer & groan on the switches,
its diner in full service, porters
spreading white sheets over the berths,
smiling, the passenger assistant coming at each meal
with reservations,
Pepin in an uproar as the Super looms closer to Ottawa,
Roberts eating his quotes in the Globe & Mail,
the Super not a runaway but a train
unrescinded,
crossing the country in 4 days on schedule,
manned by rail workers
deaf to government intervention,
who are their train & run its surely,
who become their dreams

Super-Continental, 1955-1981

Finally I love even the muteness of it,
its dependence on us, its need
to be a train,
carrying passengers daily;
even its polite
standing-by, huffed up with steam
in the stations,
huge, difficult to caress, comfort-

Hard to step thru its doors & know
that next week there won't be a train
Hard to tell why we failed
not knowing   Why
Walking away from diner & sleepers into another job
Our craving, nearly sexual
unheard
To want the ugliness of it, the metal
skin & bolts holding it together, steam-pipes
dirty as ever,
generators humming under the floor,
tables set for dinner, thrust
of diesel power pushing speed

I love its ugliness as a thing with soul,
as a possible human painted blue,
as transport to destinations
we dream of, its cars bring us,
courtesy & service,
the myth of strangers meeting
as words jump from their shoulders like desire
& now sorrow,
the Super-Continental unheard, voted down
in parliament
The crossings & mainline empty of it,
the talk of passengers, their outbursts of
love, a muteness, unheard

14 November 1981

Certain Words, A Garden

I am a terrorist in my life,
each morning arrives again to me
holding the accident of birth, a blanket, my mother's
deep sighing.
To get up, cherished, & not cry out to anything,
neither wet doors, the shorn corridor,
odour of cabbages caught against the stair
Refusing to trust in the talk
of pistols, its grimness deafens a whole garden,
breeds sentinels on the roofs of buildings, feigned
relaxation, dedication, fear
Instead to dress quietly in the old coat & my usual shoulders,
empty of ancestors,
rejecting the innocence of age, the white step
of the fou with his crumpled ass
& nightgown

After all night throwing knives against
the kitchen table,
against the lampshade that spoke your name,
you catch yourself, ticking, certain words.
You touch the holy palms
brought by your accidental brothers, given to you,
hold them free of the
ceremonies.
In the morning, now, the neighbours
hear you laughing

because the law is a gone story
awaiting apprehension, because it is not enough
to sell your furniture;
your life alone has reached you, captive, stubborn:
in its arms at last
your terror rises
with red wings & a lonely heartbeat, & your voice
opens up a whole garden

If Only

If only Christ *would*
stand visibly, as they said he would,
above the sorrowing grasses, the earth often
eating their soft stems,
the battered hulks of cars & cigarettes,
the trip in summer under orange headlamps
of a freeway,

with the whole family, Father
driving with his large hands curled
upon the wheel,
his children crying in the back seat, the prairie,
or Calgary, where they stopped
in a parking lot, where the children

watched the firemen put out
blazes in grocery carts, & in young boys' dreams.
Who live there day after day:
one of them is my brother, learning
to count money, to stroke white paint on the walls
of new buildings,
to console his parents who never picture
where he goes, or why his mouth
is so dry, why

grocery carts have stopped burning, the family
turned & gone home,
having already been somewhere, long enough
without even seeing my brother
or touching his stiff white hands, kissing his blue
mouth vacant & charming: or hearing him speak -
In the language of money that he knows well

& tells no one; how, when he rides the last
bus to the end of the city,
he sees Christ stand visibly in the dirt, where
the boys burnt the prairie in a long line of orange flame,
killing him, taking his soft heart up
in their bloody arms

Woman At Phaistos

A woman on the way to Phaistos,
she is   as light is
to the road, she   makes it navigable.
Hard grey boots, bare-legged,
head swabbed in a shirt,   she hikes against
the sun's burning/   Obstinate

She navigates gladly   the road we imagine,
its blind hills, white leaf,
rock   plains & greenhouses

We too, her lovers, listen   to the ruined city she searches,
wind pulls
the salt thread of silence from its stones.

Who were they, women of Phaistos, bent over
the fruit-press in the walls of stone palaces...
Who was the last one? Did she know
what she was leaving?

We too, unanswered: watch the woman who is our lover
on the road-edge walking, slightly
Arabic with her shirted head & moving,

            She listens
& hears only the sun that turns
our dream to ashes
It is not the stones   that drown her
but the cars & buses passing to Galini,
that strand her in history, where she wants to be,
human as
            a whisper,
            a fluffed heartbeat,
            weird packet of feeling, & bone

Apocalypse, For Spencer

for Stanley Spencer, R.A.

There is no memory but
what has fled,
            scaling the fences.
The angels of the apocalypse are   housewives
after all, well-printed, dusting chairs

There are forms that begin &
begin   again, houses that lift their curtains
skyward
Heads that pull up slowly into apples
Muscles gripping arms
Cowls that call to Christ   out of the silent beam of sky
mended with wood, his sighs

An ordinary fact of the street, like
the saint in his dressing gown, head tipping the roof-tiles
between houses,   preaching to hens/

White as the garments they wear,
a wall against not-existing,
the Resurrected climb out of thin graves in Cookham
onto grass so green,   kissing between their hands
The astonished stigmata
that the artist gave them, a shy passion touching
their arms & washed bodies:
Their embrace coloured gently & made
Entire,   a family